THREE SERMONS

Rev. Dr. Verne Slover

S. H. Williams,

THREE SERMONS

BY

DAVID SWING

WITH SELECTIONS AND LETTERS

REVISED EDITION

CHICAGO
1894.

DEDICATED TO THE MEMORY

OF

DAVID SWING.

The first edition of this little book was pub-
lished for private circulation with the loving consent
and co-operation of our friend and teacher, David
Swing. Now that his dear voice is forever stilled,
in love and tears and in tenderest remembrance of
the comfort and inspiration to us of all his words,
again we send forth his messages of comfort to all
who mourn.

MR. AND MRS. W. A. TALCOTT.

Rockford, Ill., December, 1894.

DEAR FRIENDS.

MR. AND MRS. TALCOTT:

Of course I can have no objection to your publishing any of my discourses which may contain some word of comfort to those who are mourning over their dead. Your own home has met with such sad losses, that if any hearts know what words are full of comfort, your hearts must be stored with that sad ability. I wish the whole public could know with what resignation and peace you have passed from the tears of the grave back to every form of human and Christian duty.

It is the mistake often of those who have lost some loved one to think that they must attempt to recover from the awful shock and separation. No educated mind ought ever to recover fully from such wounds of the spirit. When a child or near one by blood or by a divine friendship goes away from us, the mourning should continue while life lasts. Are we to suppose that Edmund Burke ever forgot for a day the death of his son? Did Hallam feel for a few months only the absence of his idolized boy? The tears must last while the absence continues. Nothing but the meeting in immortality should end the long pensive remembrance. The sad memories which death brings are a part of our education. Under that influence of an absent soul the heart softens, and man goes forth each day more of a friend to his race, and more of a worshiper of his God. The death of a friend exalts those who remain to weep.

But this grief must not interfere with the duties and noble pursuits of our world. Sorrow must ennoble duty, not end it. Earth's blossoms must still be beautiful even after they have wreathed a dead forehead. We must so feel that death is a part of God's plan and God's love, that the grave of a lost one must seem attached to the work we are to do while we remain in these sunbeams. These tombs and these duties are entangled. We cannot separate them. Our sorrows, our joys and our duties are inseparable. We cannot put asunder what God has thus joined. May all who mourn have such a faith in the teachings of our common religion that each absent one may make duty more sacred, happiness higher and deeper, and heaven nearer.

With much love,

Yours as ever,

DAVID SWING.

Chicago, February 23, 1891.

CONTENTS

———

GOD CARES FOR OUR DEAD

"GOD is caring for all our dead. They go from us, but not from Him."

—*Swing*

GOD CARES FOR OUR DEAD

Thou shalt not muzzle the ox when he treadeth out the corn. Is it for the oxen that God careth? or saith he it wholly for our sake?

—I Corinthians ix. 9.

The Mosaic law was cheered not a little by sunny spots of benevolence. The advance of the virtues and amenities has not been with equal step. Soldiers, under severe discipline, march with an even front; but when men or children are crossing a field on a holiday, no line of advance is observed. Some run, some attempt to walk the most slowly possible. The virtues thus advance. The movement is informal. Some forms of good are running far in advance of the other forms. Some are far along toward perfection, while other forms of culture or love are in the first stages of life.

Thus some parts of the old Hebrew laws were full of wrath, while other parts were rich in mercy. A rebellious child must be stoned to death; an infidel must be killed; a witch must not be permitted to live; a slave might be whipped to death; but in contrast with such bloody statutes lay the laws that some figs and grapes and bunches of wheat should be left for the poor who should glean the fields after the harvest; that all men and domestic animals should rest one day in seven; that no young man should be called upon to go to war in the first year after his wedding; and every eighth year was to be one long holiday for the fields, and the men and animals which toiled on the land. At the end of every seventh year came this magnificent vacation for all the rural populace. "Bloody Moses" was also kind and loving Moses in some hours. The oxen which were compelled to go round and round, tramping out the wheat, must not wear muzzles. They must be permitted to have their mouths full of the new straw and new grain. As they had plowed the field and had helped in all things between the seed time and the reaping, it was but justice that when the thresh-ing day had come the ox might take up a mouthful of the sweet stuff. The Mosaic age was cruel, but it was illumined by bright spots.

St. Paul said this law of oxen came from God to Moses; but not on account of the oxen at all, but only to typify through those dumb brutes God's care for man. Paul said: Does God care for oxen? He gave the law for man's sake alone.

It is much to be regretted, perhaps, that the Pauls and the St. Johns were not made immortal, so that we could, at any time, ask them what they meant by certain words and phrases. Paul's Greek, "He made the law wholly (*pantos*) on account of us," needs some explanation, for our age does not feel that God exhausts his regards upon man, and cares nothing about the condition of the ox. Our period thinks of an infinite love, and knows that after God has cared for the human family there is some solicitude left for the great animal world.

Moses and Paul have at least furnished to us an illustration of the care that envelops the human race. In the autumn days when out in the open air, upon the good, dry, earthen threshing-floor, the oxen were separating the wheat from the straw, God stood by to order that no muzzle should come between the mouth and the food. That law came more directly from heaven than other of the Hebrew statutes. It carries the marks of a divine and perpetual goodness. It possesses a beauty that will never fade. If in our egotism we assume that

God Cares for our Dead.

heaven loves us more than it loves the brute kingdom, our weakness is pardonable, for the Bible itself
says a man is of more value than many sparrows.
God cares for man.

What a deep and sweeping truth it is when any-
body or any creature cares for us! And if this
great scene is all perfected by the fact that God also
cares for us, then what a world we have in which to
live and die!

When philosophers have attempted to define
civilization, they have come short as often as they
have attempted to fashion it out of learning or art
or law or politeness, but when, at last, they begin to
mix into the crucible the element of care for all
other mortals, and for all forms of life, they reach
a more perfect definition. Civilization is more of
the heart than of the mind. At least the powers of
the mind are most valuable when they inflame the
soul. If one cannot possess both learning and
kindness, he would better pray for the kindness.
Cicero said, " Friendship can make riches splendid."
Friendship can plan and do so many things for its
wealth to execute. It can plan a good winter even-
ing for a group, and it can plan an afternoon for a

hundred children. It can roll in a Christmas log for a larger hearth. It can spread happiness to the right and left. It can spend money most beautifully and make gold shine. But what is friendship but another name for that care which in the Mosaic age left some sheaves in the field and some grapes in the vineyard.

We are all so accustomed to the great atmosphere of friendship that we live unconscious of its worth. When a man has suddenly lost his good name he realizes what it once was to have the world love him. He did not know until that black hour what a happiness lay in the common good mornings spoken to him in the street. Viewed from the new disgrace, each smile from a business man, a woman, or a child seems to have been richer than a bed of violets. Man could, perhaps, bear the loss of his own love of others, but he cannot bear the thought that all have ceased to love him. Reared in this climate of kind regard, man little realizes what a vernal air it is. Gentle as our material atmosphere is in action, it presses with a force of fourteen pounds upon the square inch. It is not felt by even a rose leaf or a butterfly's wing, because, being a fluid, it presses equally in all directions. No cheek of infant feels its weight. Just so gentle is the common esteem that encompasses the human race. It is more powerful in highly civilized lands, but in the pagan nations it exists and makes the Chinaman worship the very bones of his ancestors, and makes the exile wish to return and die in his native land. He wishes even his grave to be cared for by relatives and friends. To care for others is benevolence and love; to be cared for is the desire of all human nature.

The play of King Lear illustrates the dreadful lot of that heart which has fallen out of the world of regard. Avarice and wicked intrigue closed against the king all the doors which had once swung open at love's touch. The awful storm in the woods at night which beat upon the head, not only uncrowned but uncared for and white with old age, is a fit emblem of the darkness and tempest in the spirit when its friends are all lost. Cordelia stands beautifully for that loving care which creates the vital air which all souls must breathe that they may live. The Greek drama taught the same sacred lesson in the Antigone who stood by her

blind father when all other human beings had deserted him. The more cruel became the world's
neglect, the nearer the daughter drew to the friend-
less OEdipus. After the lightning and the awful
thunder had slain the father, then the loving girl
reappeared in the heroic act of caring for the dead
body of her brother, which body a despotic king
had ordered to be made food for the swine and the
vultures. Thus, the English genius and the Greek
genius, living more than two thousand years apart,
saw with equal clearness the beauty of a world
where many care for each one, and the deep misfortune of the being for whom no one cares. Past
fame and past empire offer no consolation to the
heart which says, "No one cares for me." If the
Greek Antigone is the best woman that has ever
been seen upon any stage, ancient or modern, it is
chiefly because she stands for the most powerful of
all truths and thoughts,—some one cares deeply for
me.

The reformers of all the lowest classes expect
many a ruined mind to awake and rise in a new
life when it is touched by this magic wand of outside esteem. *fraternalism* The abandoned boy or girl becomes

ambitious for good as soon as either learns that kind eyes are watching and praying. While there is no chemistry that can weigh and measure sentiments, it seems probable that the thought, " I love another," is not so inspiring as the thought that another loves me. Whether this emotion comes in childhood or in old age, or in that youthful hour which is the most deeply covered with all the vines and blossoms of sentiment, it is perhaps the most influential thought which lives within the spirit's temple. When Marquette revealed his care for the Indians, they became transformed. No red man in the mountains, no negro in Africa or in foreign bondage, can resist the power of this solicitude. It undermines like a wave; it rends like an earthquake; it melts like a fire; it inspires like music; it binds like a chain; it detains like a good story; it cheers like a sunbeam.

When great criminals have been detected in their career they all grieve that their mothers shall now know the truth; grieve, not because they love their mothers, but because the mothers love them; that her admiration can follow them no more. That esteem, present in all the days of infancy, ever present in manhood, assumed still all through the period of time, must now cease as an admiration, and exist only as a pity and a grief. This truth and consolation that some fellow-beings are caring for us is thus reaching upward from where the oxen are treading out the wheat, to where man is passing life as a poor laborer, as a rich man or as a king. No heart can escape it. The inference is, therefore, that all the forms of life are deserving of some one's regard. It is not only your happiness to be cared for by others, but it is also your right. The right to light, air and liberty is not more real than this right to a share in the great omnipresent solicitude. It is not a right which one would care to present before a legislature for the purpose of securing a law, or before a court for the purpose of securing a decision, but still it is a right which not only envelops infancy and the barefoot school-boy, but also all the manhood and womanhood upon our globe. It is very silent, but very real.

In all our admiration and study of material nature we are all struck by the one defect present everywhere, in hill and valley, rainbow and dewdrops, sky and ocean, cataract and meadow brook,—a

defect carried in each golden cloud, borne along
in each perfumed wind, hidden in the leaves of
each rose, where the trees rise to the height of
three hundred feet, where the rocks rise in sub-
limity, and the natural garden below lies in the
beauty of a terrestrial paradise, there lies this defect
of nature, never absent from a city, or a star, the
defect that nature does not care for you. Nature
is unable to care for man. The hills in spring or
autumn will not speak to you; the flowers are
beautiful but heartless. They would as soon deco-
rate man's grave as his cradle. The hand of the
bride and the bosom of the dead are both one and
the same to the violets. According to the rich
eloquence of William Wirt, the wife of Blenner-
hasset wept on her lovely island, tears which her
own house could not pity, tears which, in the
winter's wind, "froze as they fell." While the
exiles are journeying to Siberia or are passing long
years in a living death, the forms and forces of
nature have never come with a sympathetic word
or deed. Home and exile are one with it. Often
while a ship load of people is sinking in the ocean,
the sun is smiling sweetly on the waters, and the

"countless smiles of the sea" are playing on in presence of weeping faces that will wear no smile again forever. Roses grow red and fragrant on the dust of our dead.

The dominating care which so creates and charms humanity must, therefore, have come from some source apart from material nature, and must be expected to approach man through some intellectual or spiritual gate. It must come from something that can form attachments, that can pity, love, and express these emotions. It must, thus, come from mind to the thrashing oxen and to the higher mind of man. The universe must possess something that can care for all that lives and can suffer. The summer does not wish to come to our world; the orange does not wish to ripen; the flowers do not wish to be fragrant; the apples do not wish to grow red and sweet; the air does not wish to be changed into music; the autumn woods do not desire to be beautiful. The wish is elsewhere. There must be a great Care that is detached from nature, a sympathy that belongs to an intellectual life, a Care that makes nature its instrument and language. Some heart is back of the scene.

The relations of man to the lower forms of animal life bear witness to the fact of some omnipotent regard and to man's need of that regard. It is not man's vanity which makes him say, my horse or my dog loves me. He could say, I love my horse or my dog; but that form of expression would not be so far-reaching and pathetic as the truth and feeling that some creature loves him. Man can love the hills or love music, but the hills and music cannot love him in return. What touches the heart most is the thought that it is cared for. Therefore, said the Great Shepherd, " My sheep hear my voice." " They follow me." Henri-Frederic Amiel says in his journal, " Nothing will induce my cat to leave me. She has followed me from room to room all the day. A look, a word gratifies him." Amiel also says, " If man were what he ought to be he would be adored by all the domestic animals;" thus reminding us that man thinks much of all the kind regards sent him from the brute world. He wishes the birds and beasts to lend him their good wishes. Man seems to be the needy one. In the little poem written by Catullus to the dead sparrow of a girl, the virtues of the bird lay in its devotion to the girl. It knew the girl as well as the girl knew her mother. It fluttered around the girl's head; it nestled in her bosom; it chirped for her alone. Catullus mourned that such a sympathizing creature had gone from the world by that "path along which no life can return." Similar virtue had Ovid's parrot and Virgil's oxen. The charm was not that man loved them, but that they loved man. In an old engraving called "The Doves," the birds are revealing the greater part of the attachment. They are on the head, the shoulders, the hands, and around the feet of the ideal girl. They cared for her.

Whoever will read all these poems of the world and study all those pictures will find that the theme in the lessons is that man dwells upon the star which needs sympathy as much as it needs sunlight; and that he accepts of the attentions of the humblest creatures, not because he is an egotist, but because he is the victim of a mighty sorrow. When Pascal said that "All animals die, but man is the only animal that knows that it will die," the only animal that looks far forward to that strange event, he touched upon the fact that man is forever in need

of helping hands and voices. Humanity plays and
laughs, and yet its oceans and continents are not
half as large as its griefs. It has lived encompassed
by a black cloud. When Justice Miller lay stricken,
a distinguished man went up to the home of the
failing judge to bear love and hopes, but the visitor
died before the great jurist himself passed away.
Last summer a family, all bound together by love,
made a journey of pleasure from the South to the
New England coast. When in sight of the blue
ocean, and when all hearts were glad, they were
overtaken by one of earth's hidden calamities, and
suddenly six of the household had gone from this
world. No merit, no friendship, no beauty, no
attachments availed to keep them in this life upon
earth. For thousands of years this mystery of
death has been pursuing mankind, mowing down
the living, thinking, and loving children as autumn
leaves. Death contemplates still other campaigns.
He contemplates a forward movement which will
make this generation all pass away from the world
it so loves. Death loves history more than he loves
poetry ; his sculpture is all monuments of the past ;
his favorite piece of ground is " God's acre ; " his

favorite time is the night; his favorite music is a
dirge; his color is black.

Man may be great in mind, in skill, or in wealth,
and yet his situation is most pathetic. All that
pathos which is so precious in music comes into art
from the pathos in man's life. The tears in music
relate it to humanity. All hearts love it because
it weeps with them. We cannot say to music,
"We have mourned and you would not lament."
It has no will of its own. It does nothing but
blend with the pensiveness of the soul.

Humanity thus is asking for sympathy. Education does not cure its pain; rather it doubles it and
makes the condition of man more pitiful to a cul-
tured mind than it is to an unlettered Indian. With
the deepening of civilization the cry will deepen,
Who cares for man? Who will help him? Is
there some great sympathy in which he lives and in
which he will die? Is there some love above these
elegant forms of life, saying, "Thou shalt not
silence the heart that is threshing the grain of this
world. Is there some higher law passed for man?
Thou shalt not reward the ear with deafness nor the
eye with blindness, nor love with death." Perhaps

that law of the threshing floor expands and takes in all of us children who would gladly fill our mouths with the fresh harvest of a second life.

This the student of our world perceives,—that while nature has no sympathy for man, while the ocean would as soon drown a child as float a log, yet through this same nature there beams a solicitude not its own. Some mind wishes the fruits to ripen for man, the birds to sing for him, and for him the great scenes of utility and beauty to pass along in their marvelous procession. A very large part of all the visible things from the stars to the soil of the field speaks in tones of sympathy, and says, Some one cares for man. Each useful thing, each happy thing, each beautiful thing is a word in the great language of helpfulness, and all joined together they make an eloquent plea within the blessed field of optimism. The situation of man is peculiar in this, that all the surrounding air pities his misfortunes. Not the air, indeed, but something that works in it and through it. As on the dangerous shore of the stormy sea great lights shine all night long, because they are fed and guarded by some human anxiety, thus man in his shadowed years beholds many lights of love that are lighted and guarded by a hand unseen.

In the painter's landscape there is always demanded some form of life,—a lamb, a bird, a domestic animal; because these can care for man. Thus the cattle become greater than the meadows. In one of Emerson's little poems the squirrel is greater than the mountain. In Dante's vast work, the celestial forest is less touching than the birds which, through the woods of Chiassi, rolled their gathering melody. In such a world there is some care greater still behind these little forms of life and love; a love-sun of which all other sympathies are only the reflected rays, as the clouds are often touched with a light that has not fully come. In the gigantic landscape of humanity there must be seen the living form of God. His foot-prints must be seen in the hills; His divine song must be heard in the summer and autumnal branches.

Last May, when that rich month was hurrying toward the greater wealth of June, death claimed suddenly one from this congregation; one of the greatest minds and one of the kindest hearts that even our good age ever gives to any one of its hildren. When the coffin had been lowered into the earth, and religion and love had joined in the final amen, many strong men were reluctant to leave the place and desert the form that had, for long years, been near in such manly magnificence. Such a being did not seem made for the tomb. He seemed too great for such a rest in the ground. But as the living group turned away from the scene, one thought came to all,—God cares for our dead.

Falling statesman, sinking friend, dying woman, pale, sleeping child, pass from human sight, but only to fall into that divine, tender solicitude which is hidden from us by the rich but heavy curtains of nature. The perpetual exodus from our homes, our church, our fields of common friendship, is to be explained only by the great invitation that comes to the dying from some better land. As they all came into this being by a Creator's goodness, by the path of that goodness they all depart.

> Who leads through trackless space the stars of night?
> The power that made them guards them still;
> They know Him not, yet, day and night,
> They do His perfect will;
> Unchanged by age,
> They hold on high
> Their pilgrimage
> Of glory round the sky.

43451

Go, meditate with man among the tombs,
And there the end of all things view;
Visit, with man, spring's earliest bloom
And see all things made new;
Thence rapt, aloof,
In ecstacy,
Hear, from heaven's roof,
Stars preach eternity.

GONE BEYOND THE VEIL

"THERE are voices before you, outreaching hands, loved ones waiting. When the time shall come for you to die, you will go from this world more willingly."

—*Swing*.

GONE BEYOND THE VEIL

Go to now, ye that say: To-day or to-morrow we will go
into this city and spend a year there, and trade and get
gain: whereas ye know not what shall be on the morrow.
What is your life? For ye are a vapor that appeareth
for a little time and then vanisheth away. For ye ought
to say: If the Lord will, we shall live and do this or that.
                                                —*James* iv. 13.

The savage tribes do not keep any record of
their seasons and personal birthdays. The early
Indians of our continent kept some rude records of
events the most prosperous or adverse. The moon
was generally their unit of measurement. The sun
was not so evident in his movements. The moon,
which at times grew full in the face and then waned,
was the most available clock for all those wild men
who occupied this continent for unreckoned years.
Each separate day was a fragment too small to be
counted, and the movements of the sun north of
the equator were beyond the red man's grasp. It
is not probable any of the uncivilized races ever
paid much regard to the exact age of an individual.
We were young, now we are old, was a statement

exact enough to suit the chieftains who had seen many moons and many hunting seasons and many battles. It is certain that with them, as with the negroes, their personal record of age was often ten or twenty years away from the truth.

The more exact measurement of time could not have come at the demand of commercial interests alone, nor at the command only of that intellect which loves to measure exactly all objects, but the effort must have been stimulated not a little by the joy or soberness of that kind of knowledge which tells each one how long he has been in the world. The moment mental culture came man began to count more carefully his summers and winters; and when the mind had become brilliant enough to compose the ninetieth psalm, it had become so proud or sad over life that it could say, " The days of our years are three score years and ten." In the culture which adorned the classic lands each one numbered carefully his years, but the months and days were seldom written down. Socrates died at 70, Sophocles at 90, Demosthenes at about 60. With the expanse of literature and all thought and feeling, the month and day began to appear in the record. Life grew more precious as it ran. Virgil died on the 22d of September, 19 B. C., in his 51st year; Horace died on the 19th of November, in the 8th year, B. C., at the age of 57. Augustus Cæsar died August 19, 14 B. C. Such details we must not ascribe to more exact astronomy or to better timepieces, but to the growing appreciation of the greatness and marvel of existence. One might think the exactness of count came from the desire of the mercantile world to be true to its contract, were it not for that solicitude which marks the minute even when a loved one falls into the last sleep. The more man thinks, the more strange becomes every single fact in the incident of death.

The close of a year cannot but bring to us all the half-sad thought that our visit to this earth is drawing nearer and nearer to its close. To the youngest this reflection cannot so reasonably come, but soon after one has passed the middle line, the meditation reappears whenever the autumn leaves strew the ground, and whenever the Christmas festival has passed by. Much depends upon the sensibility of the heart, for when Bryant was only eighteen years old, he said to the world there

Comes a still voice — Yet a few days and thee
The all-beholding sun shall see no more
In all his course, nor yet in the cold ground
Where thy pale form was laid with many tears,
Nor in the embrace of ocean, shall exist
Thy image.

The Author of life and death so laid His plans that youth itself is always kept under the shadow of that impending night. As though the mind would be wisest when it were most sober, and would be most kind when most humble, God ordered that no thoughtful person would ever dare say, " I shall live another year; older persons will die, but I shall live." Of one million who look out of the windows in infancy, and point to the moon and stars as so many toys within easy reach, in thirty years four hundred thousand have passed from the doors and the windows. Five hundred thousand have gone before the fiftieth year has come. For mental, and, perhaps, religious reasons, the Author of humanity has made all minds which are capable of thought move along in the midst of the one-thrilling uncertainty. It may, perhaps, deepen a little when white hairs have come, but the shadow is a great one, able to becloud not a little the sky of each.   As the twilight in the summer touches all objects alike, tree and grass, valley and mountain, subduing the green of the meadows and the gaudy poppies in the wheat, spreading a veil over the lakes and rivers, taking away the spots and flaunting plumes of the birds, thus the fact of mortality is a widespread eventide which dims the color of gold, of fame, of ambition, and subdues not a little the lustre of Beauty's eye and the roses on her cheek.   This eventide of death is as old and broad as human reflection.   We cannot go back in history far enough to find a spot where the grave is not playing its part in soliloquy and in all public literature.   Cicero said, "Death may come to-day. It is always hanging over us like the stone over Tantalus."   Tibullus said, "Why should men kill each other in war?   Soon enough would they all go to that black region where there are no fields of wheat, no trailing vines?"   It is a pressure as extensive and as uniform as that of the atmosphere, but a weight of sadness.

Reports often come to us of persons who, in full health and prosperity, express a willingness to give up this existence.   A very large majority of these persons are insincere. Their words are not the pictures of facts, but only the sketches drawn by untaught fancies. Should death offer his services nearly all of this multitude would plead some reason for his delay. This world and the human heart are wonderfully entangled. Often when a youth or an adult must only change his nation or move away from places made dear by childhood, tears fall. The heart is attached to each being and each object.

When the twenty-five early years have passed by, the soul finds itself chained to all objects, the greatest and the least. The boys who used to hunt in the thickets and woods for the wild blue-grape, often found the grapes far up in the top of a great tree. It was then the resolve of youthful vandalism to cut off the vine at the ground, and then by the power of a dozen hands detach it from the oak or the beech. It leaves its old home with reluctance, for it has wound itself around many branches, and the tendrils of the vine have established long and strong friendships with the twigs and boughs. When, at last, the vine falls to the earth the air is full of the leaves and grapes which are detached by the thoughtless violence. Each torn leaf, each grape in the shower was a tear over the cruelty of the separation. Thus the heart becomes attached in youth to its home and native land, and, if it must remove over the mountains, or over the sea, then does it reveal its sweet entanglements, and its removal recalls in the sad soul the memory of the vine and its giant tree.

But if the mind is thus wedded to its farm or home or country, with what language can we describe man's attachments to his life in this world? In addition to the indescribable instinct of life which man shows together with all the dumb animals, there exists a most marvelous mental enchainment of the mind to this world. When man thinks of parting with the sun and moon, with winter and summer, with all that is good and beautiful in nature, and with his friends and home and loved ones, then does he betray a solemnity and sadness which no language can portray. It is seldom any educated being in good health of body lives without these gold fetters and is willing that this day should be the last.

All persons ought to love very deeply this world,

because, made by an infinite power and wisdom, it
should be confessed to be a home worthy of its
Creator,—a place marked by the infinite. The
earth should seem a part of a tremendous plan,
and each day on its bosom should seem a day
spent amid beauties and wonders. Has any mind
ever been too great for this terrestrial hour? Has
any statesman been too wise for the need of the
people? Has any art excelled the sunset or the sea,
or equaled its own ideals. Has any one sung too
sweetly for our planet? Has any orator uttered
the truth too truly and too well? Has civilization
exhausted all high motives and performed its high
duties? Has wealth become too benevolent? Has
each man become the brother of all men? Have
the flowers lost their color? Has the next June
ceased to haunt the chambers of Hope? What an
infinite world! And why should any child of mortality wish to go from this world to-day or to-morrow? The wisdom and power of God meet here
to chain man's foot to this earthly shore. Man is
not foolishly attached to his life; he is divinely
bound. Great friendships, great duties, and noble
purposes make man seem a part of the very world
itself.

Notwithstanding these many and powerful chains, yet each human being must, in the plan of God, be taken from this globe. Man does not willingly go; he is taken. As an unseen force made the suns and the planets, and covered all or some of the planets with verdure and life, as an unseen force placed man here, so that power comes in some unknown manner and separates man's soul from his body. The God of the beginning is the God of the end. It is not that man goes, but that God comes. Man is not an independent being; he is a piece of a plan.

Forbidden to be anxious to go, man is permitted to bow in philosophic submission. He must so live as not to make death self-brought. He must live as in the midst of laws which a God has enacted, and he must assume their wisdom. No law of life was passed that it might be broken, but only that it might be obeyed. While any child of mortality is standing amid all the laws, duties, and pleasures of the world, it need not be willing, indeed, to go out of this life; but should the order come, it may well be submissive, as though the God of nature were present in person in the summons. The greatness

of the summons may make the order read the more
sweetly to the heart. In the world of the atheist
such submission would seem more difficult. There
is no divine voice in the last hour. But, as we are
not in this temple in the name of atheism, we need
not plan for it a philosophy of the tomb.

All that the sojourner of time can do is not to
trifle with his life, not to expose a delicately
wrought frame and mind to the rudeness of any
vice. As the palm tree must obey the laws of its
structure, and cannot be transplanted into the North-
ern zone, so man must live in obedience to the laws
of his body and soul. He must stand encompassed
by the ways and means appointed by nature, the
physical and spiritual ways of wisdom, and then
come when death may, it will be the simple voice
of God, and submission will be within the spirit's
reach. The sinking life needs nothing so much as
the feeling that it "has done what it could, it has
attempted to live according to the laws of the body
and the mind, it has carried carefully over land and
sea, amid rock and amid flowers, the delicate urn of
life. It has done what it could."

All of the great Greeks found a final peace in

the thought that death was only the call of the supreme God. In the drama of Œdipus, this theory of the divine presence plays its powerful part. Antigone had long been leading by the hand her blind father the exiled king. When at last they had sat down in a sacred place, the daughter was allured a few steps away from her idolized parent, and while she was thus detained there was a vivid flash of lightning and an awful thundering. When the daughter trembled with these sounds, and had, perhaps, heard the mysterious, invisible chorus saying, "How terribly the thunder rolls around," she ran toward the sacred place, but, in that tumult, her father had passed away from the world. She and the king had sat down where the bay tree, the olive, and the vine mingled and were full of nightingales; but into that sweet bower death had come, not as a deformity, but as a sublime uprising of the entire scene. All was transfigured. The death was in harmony with the olive trees, the thunder in full accord with the songs of the birds, and life and death were one. The father and daughter, united or separated, were one, because all the scene came alike from the same God. In God all the details met.

This repose in Greek philosophy reappears in that of Jesus Christ, only in the religion of Jesus the love surpasses the display of simple power. The awful thunder disappears, and the olive trees remain in a more silent beauty. The Greek force is lost in the Christian goodness. Now God, as the hymn says, " Lets the lifted thunder drop," and " Jesus weeps and loves me still." The nightingales still sing in the bay trees, in the olives, and the vines; nothing being absent except the terrific thunderings.

The exit from this existence is made the more peaceful by its universality. If some few mortals were to be exempt from death, we should all be filled with daily anxiety as to whether we were to be among the doomed ones. In the decree which declares that all, all must die, there is whispered to each heart many a word of peace. The past centuries with their once happy millions, now all dust, with their kings and subjects, the rich and the poor, the learned and the unlettered, with their Homers and their Cæsars, their apostles and their martyrs, all in one wide grave, silence all the rising protests in the hearts now living, and make every head bow and repeat softly the words, " I know that I too must go the way whence I shall never return." In the inevitable there is peace.

The immensity of the human race far back of us, its absence now, the marks of its chariot wheels in the streets of Pompeii, the work upon its statues and Corinthian columns of hands that are now motionless, the poems of a Virgil who is not here, the annals of a Julius Cæsar whose armies no longer march, the crusaders who are no longer moving proudly toward Palestine, the paintings of the Sistine Chapel from whose splendor the artist has gone away, the homes of Shakespeare and Scott long since deserted by their occupants, the entire seventeenth century, which, holding in its hands the new destiny of the human mind, is not here to wear upon its forehead a single wreath of the now living gratitude, all combine to proclaim the breadth of that avenue which leads the human millions forever from their earthly homes. Its breadth amounts to a grandeur. The isolated soul of the nineteenth century need not shrink from obeying the call to journey along the road so full of human footprints, and, for the most part, so bordered with altars erected to the name of God.

The resignation to go whither all the past has journeyed is made more perfect by the thought that along this dignified and almost magnificent highway many of the friends of each one now living have already gone. One by one, for ten, or twenty, or a half hundred years, the loved ones have been passing out of sight, going in the power of manhood or womanhood, or in radiant youth or in childhood's innocence.

When man has reached seventy the friends who have passed away are more in number and in sacredness than those who remain. As in the late September the blossoms in garden and field are only a few compared with those whose leaves caught the sun and showers of midsummer, thus man standing on the extreme confine of his life notes that the near ones on earth are but a few compared with those who, to friendship's roll-call, would have to answer from the fields of heaven.

To this philosophy of resignation, which has comforted all the civilized lands of all ages, Christianity adds only additional power and charm. It does not harm the submission which mankind had before it came, nor does it take away what peace in

God the mind may possess which has not accepted of a revelation. It is only a vast accession to the bulk of human life,— an answer to the longings of all who have stood amid the mysteries of life and death. Christ did not come to oppose the hope of a Socrates or an Aurelius, but to increase its influence in the later hearts. Our sun differs from a twinkling star only in being nearer. The sun is so near that our planet exults in its light and heat. Thus, before Christ, heaven was made dim by an awful distance; after Him it drew nearer, and seemed to reveal to many eyes its sapphire gates. The stream of the Bible empties into the general river of religious thought, and makes it flow toward eternity with redoubled volume. Under the leadership of Jesus of Nazareth, the subsequent centuries have thought more ardently and more wisely about the possibilities beyond the grave. In that spiritual awakening reason also was aroused, and with the deepening of thought came a more general feeling that man was to pass from this life to a better world. Christ has been at once a leader of reason, of piety, and of hope.

And yet, although for thousands of years mankind has pondered over this phenomenon of death, it retains its awful solemnity and checks all the egotism of the thoughtful mind. St. James says: "Oh, how foolish is man. He says: 'I will go into the city and spend a year there and get gain,' whereas he does not know what shall be on the morrow." But St. James understated the real truth, for the little child also says: "To-morrow I shall play with my cousin or my schoolmate;" and behold the child is buried on the morrow, and its toys are on its tomb. We cannot picture only the silver-haired as making these plans that fail. Upon our canvas we must paint the bride, the school-girl, the student, the infant, as overtaken by this strange storm. If you recall any noble hero of four-score years, you must see his grave as being near that of some boy who was in his first days at school, or of some girl whose cheek was rosy-red. Burke, Hallam, Lincoln followed far behind beloved children. This path is full of little footprints. For each aged one who goes to heaven, there is a group of youth to wave the welcome from the jewelled walls. Thus reaching out its arms toward old and young, the porch of the philosopher and the cradle of the infant, Death gathers us all up in its sweeping mystery, rebukes our pride, and mingles all our smiles with tears. Amazing event which only a God can fathom!

We need not dim the wonderful sunshine of these final December days with any foolish or childish weeping, but we should possess the religion and the human affection that can read over in our hearts the names of those whom the year has let fall as it has run.

The Bar Association of this city has lost eighteen of its brotherhood since last New Year's Day. Each month issued its call. January placed three under her snows; May placed two under her flowers. But the Bar Association only illustrates that greater association, society itself, to which we all belong. Composed of all ages and pursuits it makes a greater catalogue of its dead. From this church association many have passed away, some amid public lamentings, others under a shower of hidden tears. The great, the good, the kind, the generous, the young, the middle-aged, the old have alike gone. To eulogize the noble men who are absent to-day would be to slight the usefulness and infinite self-denial of the womanhood that has fallen into this sleep.

To name these daughters of God would be to slight the little children who have had to fold little hands on their innocent but dying hearts. Oratory itself would not know where to speak its kindest words, whether over the coffin of a judge or great lawyer, or over the white face of the dead child. As when a ship sails with many on board, whom we on the shore both know and love, we cannot fling many words to each one across the widening waters, as we must simply wave one farewell to all; so to-day as we see this group of exiles leaving the flowers of May, the harvests of August, and the colored leaves of autumn forever, we can only wave one farewell to all and commit them all alike to the ocean, on either shore of which lies the kingdom of God. Farewell.

The immensity of this migration of our race, the mental and moral quality of those dying generations, the thoughts they have, the hopes they cherish, the hymns they sing, the infiniteness of the soul justify the belief that man dying passes to some nobler country.

As many a day which darkly dawns
    And shadows forth a world of cares
With sudden light grows clear and bright,
    And noon a sun-gold crownlet wears,
Thus shall it be with eyes tear-wet,
    The heart shall find its Eden yet.

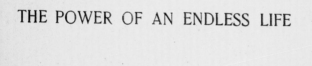

THE POWER OF AN ENDLESS LIFE

" WHAT are the associations with waters, land, flowers, clouds, grass, the perfumes of the air, compared with those ties which bind us to minds which can think and weep, and love and hope ! "

—*Swing.*

THE POWER OF AN ENDLESS LIFE

Through the power of an endless life.—Hebrews vii. 17.

Having parted company with the Hebrews, Paul very naturally made frequent attempts to justify his own course, and to induce his countrymen to imitate his example. But the Hebrews had a most strict law demanding that all priests should come from the tribe of Levi. For many centuries these high officials had thus come. In the face of such a law and such a history, Paul had adopted as the Most High Priest the Jesus from the tribe of Judah. After a long and intricate argument, little appreciated by our age, Paul reached the conclusion that Jesus was High Priest, not because of any high relationship to courtly flesh, but because of the power of an endless life. If it conferred nobility to be born a Levite and die a Levite, it ought to confer a greater honor to have an endless being, dating far back of any human tribe, and running onward without finding a tomb. The career of every Levite had been terminated by death, but the life of this new High Priest was indissoluble. He came to His office by the power of an endless life.

In the long flight of years Paul's argument about the legitimacy of priests has lost its early significance. The name and a few of the ceremonies of the priest still remain in some branches of the Christian Church, but the name and person are only a faded and dull picture of that religious scene out of which St. Paul was attempting to emerge. What remains to us of most significance is the simple phrase : "By the power of an endless life." Paul's Greek word is not the term " endless," but the term " indissoluble."

Upon an Easter Sunday there should well come an hour sacred to reflections over the idea that man is destined to live again beyond this world. It should not deter him from such reflections that he cannot prove his own immortality ; that he cannot dispel every objection and doubt, and see another life as clearly as he sees this. In all directions man experiences great difficulty in measuring himself. He does not know what mind may be, how the eye sees when its transcript of the image travels within the total darkness of the brain, how the ear hears, nor how the cells in the brain can remember and reason. A person of eighty years will remember vividly some scene or some incident that took place seventy-five years ago—the brain in the meantime having changed several times all its component parts. That mysterious brain will with ease hold countless ideas gathered from every department of knowledge, and will know quite well the date at which the information was received.

All efforts to analyze the mind and learn what it is, where it is located, how it acts in the brain tissues, have been made in vain—the greatest scientist differing but little from the prattle of an inquiring child. The inability of man to measure himself does not prove to him that he is to be reckoned an immortal, but it should prevent him from being angry or surprised over the problem of the future, and should make it absurd for him to deny that he will live once more. If a being so wonderfully made as man does not know how he came to this life, and what his life is, it is only a confirmed egotism that can profess to know that there is no hereafter for the human race. As there is no room for such egotism, so is there little room for depression on account of the absence of proof, for the darkness which envelops the soul here upon earth should make us all expect the future of man to be enveloped in a similar cloud. If man cannot see this life face to face, why should he expect any face-to-face interview with some future condition? The heart does not ask a perfect vision in some one direction when at all other compass points it is denied.

A good resolve for such an Easter morning is never to underrate the argument and hope of a second life. No heart is justified in saying more than that it is too wonderful for its power; but when eloquent lips declare that the whole doctrine of immortality is the result of the natural dreams and hopes of a fairyland they become irrational in their very effort to be the children of pure science and reason. In that little poetic episode from Mr. Robert J. Ingersoll, which begins thus:

" Life is a narrow vale between the cold and barren peaks of two eternities. We strive in vain to look beyond the heights; we cry aloud, the only answer is the echo of our wailing cry;"—

there is an error of statement which may perhaps have created or confirmed a despair for many. One of those barren peaks of the two eternities has

never sent back the echo of our wailing cry. The
"Peak" which rises up before man came to earth
has always been eloquent in loving kindness. No
heart has ever sent toward it a "wailing cry."
Science has looked toward the beginning of the
human race with all the interest which attends a
profound mystery, but it has never "wailed" as it
looked. The most joyful scene and thought is that
of the origin of the universe and its life. If over
the coming of life the morning stars sang together,
if, now, man either in his science or his poetry looks
back toward the creation as toward the most sub-
limely beautiful fact of which the mind can con-
ceive, by what law of logic or fancy is such an
amazing retrospect to be called a "wailing cry?"
Of Mr. Ingersoll's "two peaks" one of them at
least is gorgeously beautiful. But there is another
defect in the assumed gem. The eternity out of
which man came does not send back to humanity
the echo of its "wailing cry," for when man inter-
rogates the past eternity about whence he came,
that awful peak casts aside all its coldness and bar-
renness and says: Dear child, it is of no value
whence you came; you are here! It says to

Angelo: Do not wail because you do not know whence your mind came; let it fill you with joy that it reached your bosom! Thus one of these peaks instead of being adamant laughs and exults with man over the infinite beauty and reality of existence. The real truth is it is the matchless splendor of the gate through which humanity came that creates the sadness about the gate to which he goes. Life is therefore not a vale between two cold and barren eternities but a vale between two eternities, one of which possesses such measureless beauty that it compels man to think of the other only with tears.

We must, therefore, on these Easter days never underrate man's existence. Better and truer than the poetic thought of Mr. Ingersoll would be a poem which should picture man as standing between two mountain walls, one of which should be covered with verdure, song, and with the Morning angels, and should send back to all inquirers the words, "You are here in life." Before the other wall humanity might send a "wailing cry," but a sigh mingled with the hope that the God who could place man in such a beautiful valley could also get him out. Why should man see magnificence back of his race and only desolation in front? If humanity could reach this amazing world without knowing how it came, it can reach another in an unknown way.

The modern soul must be on its guard also, lest to the despairing poetry and eloquence of much American and German literature, science shall add still more of humiliation and distrust. It is common to say and feel that in presence of modern science man sinks into only one of the animal species; that he must take his position among those cellular structures which are called organic forms. But what kind of an organic form is that which can analyze all other animals, all other organisms? study them? classify them? Did the birds ever write a history of Audubon? Have the brutes ever written a history of Cuvier? Have the plants composed a history of Linnaeus? Has science, indeed, compelled man to sink to a lower place? Who made the sciences? Instead of humiliating humanity each page in modern research and discovery should take the heart further away from the common domain of nature and make it seem more the child of some distinct destiny. Instead of being only physical nature, it contemplates nature from the outside, it weighs, measures, studies, classifies and governs it. It is not in the world; it is outside of it, and looks at it.

It is a peculiarity of all the animals that they are within their world just as an angle-worm is in the ground; the fish is in the water, the bird in the air, the lion in the hot grass or hot mountains; but the fish does not examine the air, nor does the African lion study the Arctic zone or the depth of the sea. Man alone takes his stand apart from time and place, and surveys all things as a gifted spectator. He is more like a god than like the members of the simply cellular family. He is so isolated in his greatness that it may well be assumed that he carries within him an indissoluble life.

Humanity is indeed so peculiar and vast that its production by a self-acting evolution seems absolutely incredible. It would seem impossible for the dusts and fluids of earth ever to toss themselves about in such a manner as to produce living birds, trees, flowers, and, at last, man. It would first be necessary for the atoms so to toss around as to make a sun and a planet before they should begin to struggle up toward roses, humming birds, men and women. In reading this long career of the rise and progress of a handful of dust, the average heart grows incredulous and demands some Mind as standing apart from the dust atoms. The adventures of Sinbad the Sailor are much more credible than the adventures of this self-acting monad. Our logic needs most an outside mind like the intellect of man, only infinite in its power. Of such a mind man would be the child and the sharer of the Father's long life in world beyond world.

These higher estimates of man cannot betray him into personal vanity, for personal vanity always comes not from thought and truth, but from the absence of these things. Many a painted and beaded and well-feathered Indian possesses more vanity than was possible to a Newton or a Pascal. Not able to be made vain by an exaltation of itself, humanity must cling to a high self-estimate in order to escape a stricken or broken heart. We do not, indeed, need vanity, but we do all need the power of an endless life — that outlook for the mind, that great arena for the sensitive heart.

There is, in truth, a humility which ought to cry out: "What is man that God is mindful of him? the son of man that God should visit him?" It is no contradiction to say that man is capable of both humility and exaltation. When he compares himself to the Deity he may well hide in a cleft of the rock and wait for the Divine form to sweep by; but when he contemplates his place in nature he should fall upon his knees and bless his Maker for the gift of such a mind and such a soul. "What a piece of work is man! how noble in reason, how infinite in faculty; in form and moving how express and admirable; in action how like an angel, in apprehension how like a god! the beauty of the world! the paragon of animals!"

Astronomy, that science of immensity which more than the other sciences all combined overwhelms the mental faculties, should never cast a shadow upon these mortal hearts of earth. The devotees of science are fond of saying that our earth, with all its continents and oceans, is only a grain of sand upon a boundless shore. Our sun and all his system make only a dot on the field of space. The inference is, what then is man? Why should a God love him? Why should a Christ love and die for the beings upon this little globe? Thus science has of late years risen up against the assumed greatness of man. Many great and many minor intellects sink under this spell. The telescope amazes and at last depresses.

All such depression is illogical, for there is no number or vastness of worlds that can weigh anything against the dignity and exaltation of the human mind. It is now said that the greatest telescope makes it certain that from earth as a point of observation, two hundred millions of suns are now visible. Each sun is perhaps larger than the one which creates all our summer-time. But under such a revelation man need not sink, neither as an intellectual creature nor as a being beloved of God, for we cannot increase the merit of material things by increasing their volume. If man is superior to a candle he is superior to a sun, and if he transcends one sun he transcends just as easily two hundred millions of them. Suppose you pluck a leaf from an oak and compare that leaf with the mind of Plato or the heart of Jesus. All would say Plato or Christ is greater than your leaf. It will not help then your cause any to say, I shall go and bring a million leaves, and of all kinds, oak and laurel and rose. The new mountains of leaves will not change the relations of the gifted mind to the leaf. One leaf and a million leaves are all one to it. So with suns and planets; astronomy may estimate the suns at hundreds of millions and may tell of the awful spaces which light cannot cross in less than ten thousand years, but no such counting of stars affects in the least the uniqueness and grandeur of man. The mind of a child of six years of age surpasses in wonder all the suns and planets astronomers can count. It will be in vain for future students to discover a million more of fixed stars; the mind will still surpass all as it surpasses one. One and ten million suns are all the same when weighed against a rational heart. Instead of feeling that man is hidden away in a little corner of the universe, we may well feel that he rises above all physical things, however vast and numerous and however far apart. When man's mind is thought of, all distances are the same and all worlds near or far alike. If any of the other spheres transcend this globe, it will be in the mental and moral greatness in their forms of life. The size and distances of worlds will all go for naught.

When we recall what beings have lived in this planet, what minds hungry for truth, what hearts ocean-like in their kindness, what a person that One who moved across Palestine, what disciples He had, what beautiful minds there were before Jesus, and what a larger host has passed along since, what ideals have appeared on canvas, in literature, and still are hovering over each educated bosom like white doves sent from heaven, it does not seem difficult to believe that our earth with all its little-ness in the midst of infinite space may yet be a noble gem in the great moral empire of God. A little world with a soul in may be greater than large worlds desolate. The sun is a million miles in diameter. It makes a summer time, but we have it. Better the heart that has the summer time than the sun that makes it.

If little Palestine could support a Jesus Christ, why should man wonder what potency there may be in the far-off realms of space. So far as our planet is defective it draws most of its defects from

that human will which would mar as quickly all
the days and nights of the Pleiades or Orion. When
man rises in his divine might earth responds, and
each field and hill exalts him. When a noble mind
walks through a spring meadow the meadow exalts
him. The scene becomes his teacher, his poet, his
orator, his friend. There are doubtless other inhab-
ited worlds, but that they are greater or diviner
than this is not clear. This world is very eloquent
to some, and would love to be eloquent to all.
When the mind and heart walk aright, aided by
education and goodness, the field of wheat in June
turns into a matin and a vesper. A human heart
says :

" From west to east
     The warm breath blows; the slender heads droop low,
     As if in prayer.
     Again, more lightly tossed in merry play,
     They bend, and bow, and sway
     With measured beat,
     But never rest.
     Through shadow and through sun
     Goes on the tender rustle of the wheat.
     So soft and careless thrills the dreamer's ear !
     Of all that was and is, of all that yet shall be

It holds a part;
Love, sorrow, longing, pain
The restlessness that yearns,
The thirst that burns,
The bliss that like a fountain overflows,
The deep repose,
Good that we might have known but shall not know
The hope God took, the joy He made complete;
Life's chords all answer from the windswept wheat.

There might easily be a more honorable creature than man, but with difficulty could there be a better world than this. Its mountains are sublime, its violets beautiful, its tones sweet. It responds to the human wish as the harp answers with its music to the fingers. The harp stands graceful and complete in itself. It says: All depends upon the manner in which you mortals touch your hand upon my strings. You can sound discords, but you can forever and ever make me sing joyous or pathetic harmonies. By nature you cannot play my notes, but I am here to be studied, learned and loved, and then will issue from me

" Sweetest note on mortal tongue
Sweetest song by seraphs sung."

Thus stands our world very complete in powers and adaptations. It is waiting for humanity to perform its half of the divine task. When the mind does its whole duty by this little planet, its objects, from the gentlest Easter flower to the vast ocean, contribute something to its education and happiness. The scene then expands and possesses all the magnificence of a picture of God's children in God's world. But this little planet has no rewards for those who trifle with its high laws and high pursuits. However vast the universe is there cannot be a planet or a fixed star which will offer any happiness for those who, instead of making music break the harp, and instead of walking religiously, love to trample the Easter lilies under foot.

Having looked thus at man and his earth, what remains to complete the greatness of the scene? Only one thing,—that there shall lie under him in all these years the power of an endless life. He does not want nor seem to need a life which may soon dissolve. He needs the power of an indissoluble existence. Society needs the moral conception and inspiration found in the belief in immortality. Our law, our right, our charity, our friendship, our religion, our inexpressible attachment, ask for ages, not for days.

You are all justified in believing that a vision so grand and so useful will come true; you are all justified in believing that such a globe full of seasons and covered with sunbeams, full of love and thought is not simply a place in which a Christ may die, but a place from which his soul arises; you are justified in asking all the flowers of all the fields, and the spring sunbeams that make them, to assure you that under you and all whom you love flows the power of an endless life.

David Swing.

———

Born, Cincinnati, Ohio,
August 23, 1830.

Instructor in Greek and Latin
at Miami University, Oxford, Ohio,
1853 to 1866.

Pastor of Westminster, North Presbyterian,
and Fourth Presbyterian Churches,
Chicago,
1866 to 1875.

Pastor of the Central Church,
Chicago,
1875 to 1894.

Died, Chicago, October 3, 1894.

AND NOW I GO AWAY TO THE FATHER

"Wonderful as is man's coming from the Father and his coming into the world of the Father, his going away is more wonderful still; more wonderful, not because a greater event in mystery, but because it lies before us instead of behind us. To go to a heaven is really no more wonderful than to have come hither. A heaven is no more difficult than an earth. The peculiarity of death rests chiefly in the fact that it lies in the near future to each of us, and not in the mighty past, and the fact that death is my mystery, and not that of the creation of the universe. We all admit that the creation of suns and planets with their innumerable details required a God who could easily care for his children, but the grave differs from the rest of the universe in its being for you, and not long hence for you and your children. It is this personal application of death that gives it its ten-fold mystery and grief. Your grave in the grass is more tearful than the universe, because that grave is your own.

"In these moments of sad revery man must take refuge with Christ in the thought of going away to the Father. If man came from the Father, into the world of the Father, he should calmly feel that he will go away to the Father. All that man is or has came from God. Mind and soul and world came from the one source. There is not a blossom that is not of God's planting, not a stalk of wheat God did not sow. Thus, God-led into the world, and the world being that of the same God, each upright heart dying ought to say: 'And now I go away to the Father.' The divine form back of the human race, the divine laws around man's feet, should command each noble child of mortality to feel that beyond the grave there are divine arms kindly outreached."

— *Swing.*

(74)

IMMORTALITY

The most of fame goes under the grass with the other wreaths placed upon the coffin. To compose that vast and immortal thing called truth, millions of minds are consumed. There must be elsewhere a compensation for the individual thus rudely torn from life. A second life, a readjustment beyond the tomb, is the only explanation of that destroying angel which moves to and fro in our streets and homes. Society is immortal here; man is immortal hereafter. Earth consumes our great ones and our loved ones, but heaven looks down in pity and receives them to herself. Earth refines man as silver is refined—refines, but does not destroy. After the dross of the body and soul have been consumed, the spirit, thus whitened, begins elsewhere a higher life.

DAVID SWING.

We make no apology for inserting the following letters, notwithstanding the personal allusions therein contained. The sentiment they express is so germane to the purpose of this book, and they came to our sorrowing hearts with such comforting helpfulness, that we decide that we have no right to withhold them.

MR. AND MRS. W. A. T.

MY DEAR FRIEND MRS. TALCOTT:

Since the last letter from you and your husband, I have looked for some book which might set forth the beautiful solicitude of Christ over the dear little ones, but I can find nothing. It may be that no author has felt able to speak words kind enough or divine enough to be added to the words and actions of Jesus when He took up the children in His arms. Nor have I any volume that seems tender enough to be sent to your home in this day of separation. Were I with you, I should dare say but little, because all words are only an effort of the heart to express itself, and in times like yours, the effort seems vain.

You only can measure your misfortune. All the rest of the world are mute and cold. When Burke lost his son, he could not be comforted. Hallam could not. You and your husband must simply resume the duties and cheerfulness of minds that are sent here to do the will of the Infinite; but as for perfect peace, that will not come until there shall be a re-union beyond the grave.

Your loss will henceforth be a part of your character, and a part of your hope and trust. There are voices before you, outreaching hands, loved ones waiting. When the time shall come for you to die, you will go from this world more willingly. Be happy and cheerful as you were when I saw you, but do not dream of escaping from the loss. It will be lifelong, but it must not injure you but only sweeten and bless you.

Ever and ever your friend,

DAVID SWING.

March 9, '85.

(77)

LAKE GENEVA, WIS., Aug. 20, 1886.

MR. AND MRS. W. A. TALCOTT:

VERY DEAR FRIENDS,

My vacation is nearing its close, and when with more than half sad thought my heart was wondering whether these woods are not the better place for me all the year through henceforth, your letter came. I opened it while I was out under the trees. Instantly all the beauties of nature faded before the higher beauty of man, and I felt willing to go back to my duties among my fellow souls.

What are the associations with waters, land, flowers, clouds, grass, the perfumes of the air, compared with those ties which bind us to minds which can think and weep and love and hope!

I should rather sit for an hour with you both than be in a paradise which should have all things except the human heart.

I have just returned from a visit to my mother. She is in her eighty-seventh year, but does not feel their weight. Her mind is clear, and differs from our minds only in having found infinite peace. Life and death are alike to her.

* * * * * * * * * *

Ever and ever yours,
DAVID SWING.

(78)

In the wide realm of literature no words can be found which express more beautifully and adequately the thought and feeling which fill the hearts of all who knew and loved David Swing, than the classic lines written by him for the memorial services of his friend, James A. Garfield:

> Now all ye flowers make room,
> Hither we come in gloom,
> To make a mighty tomb,
>   Sighing and weeping.
> Grand was the life he led,
> Wise was each word he said;
> But with the noble dead
>   We leave him sleeping.
>
> Soft may his body rest,
> As on his mother's breast,
> Whose love stands all confessed
>   'Mid blinding tears.
> But may his soul so white
> Rise in triumphant flight,
> And in God's land of light,
>   Spend endless years.

Pure, loving and noble soul, whose life was given to the service of God, and the good of his fellowmen,—friend and brother, "Hail and farewell."

(79)

THIS BOOK WAS PRINTED
AND BOUND BY
P. F. PETTIBONE & CO.,
CHICAGO.
MDCCCXCIV.